Off to School

About Our World

Ellen Lawrence

LIGHTBOX
openlightbox.com

LIGHTBOX

Go to **www.openlightbox.com** and enter this book's unique code.

ACCESS CODE

LBG83686

Lightbox is an all-inclusive digital solution for the teaching and learning of curriculum topics in an original, groundbreaking way. Lightbox is based on National Curriculum Standards.

OPTIMIZED FOR

- ✓ TABLETS
- ✓ WHITEBOARDS
- ✓ COMPUTERS
- ✓ AND MUCH MORE!

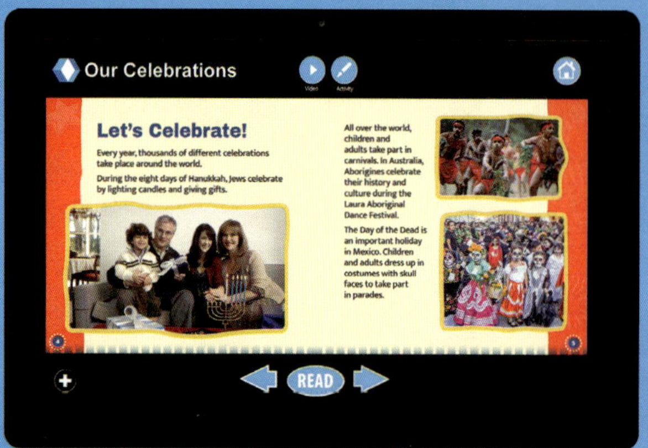

STANDARD FEATURES OF LIGHTBOX

AUDIO High-quality narration using text-to-speech system

VIDEOS Embedded high-definition video clips

ACTIVITIES Printable PDFs that can be emailed and graded

WEBLINKS Curated links to external, child-safe resources

SLIDESHOWS Pictorial overviews of key concepts

INTERACTIVE MAPS Interactive maps and aerial satellite imagery

QUIZZES Ten multiple choice questions that are automatically graded and emailed for teacher assessment

KEY WORDS Matching key concepts to their definitions

VIDEOS

WEBLINKS

SLIDESHOWS

QUIZZES

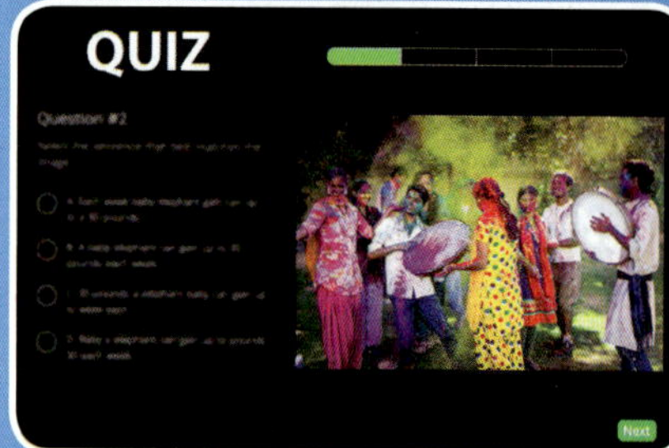

About Our World

Off to School

Off to School

It's morning, and all over the world millions of children are waking up, getting dressed, and heading off to school. They don't all get there in the same way, however.

On a school day in the United States and Canada, 30 million children ride to school on yellow buses.

Some students in Myanmar travel to and from school by boat.

Our Classrooms

Once they get to school, kids settle down to work in their classrooms. In Tanzania, some Maasai children study in a classroom that has a dirt floor and walls made out of branches.

Some boys and girls in India learn math outdoors.

A Very Tiny School

Off the coast of mainland Scotland is the tiny island of Canna. The island is home to one of the smallest elementary schools in the world. Only a few families live on Canna. So sometimes Canna School has just three or four pupils!

It takes 3 hours to travel by boat from Canna to the mainland.

Once children on Canna are 12 years old, they go to school on the mainland. Children live at the school and only go home for the weekend every two weeks.

What Do We Do at School?

We read and write and study math and science. We have fun making art. We sing, make music, and dance. We see our friends and favorite teachers.

Some children work on computers and tablets. Others do their schoolwork on a chalkboard.

The Camel Library

It's fun to go to the school library to choose a book. For some children who live in Kenya in Africa, the library has to come to them.

Many people in Kenya are nomads. They move from place to place with their animals.

Their small villages, or camps, are usually far from towns. So, a camel library visits the nomads' villages.

Three camels can carry about 200 books.

Earthquake Drills

Japan is a country that has many earthquakes. During an earthquake, the ground shakes. This can cause terrible damage to buildings.

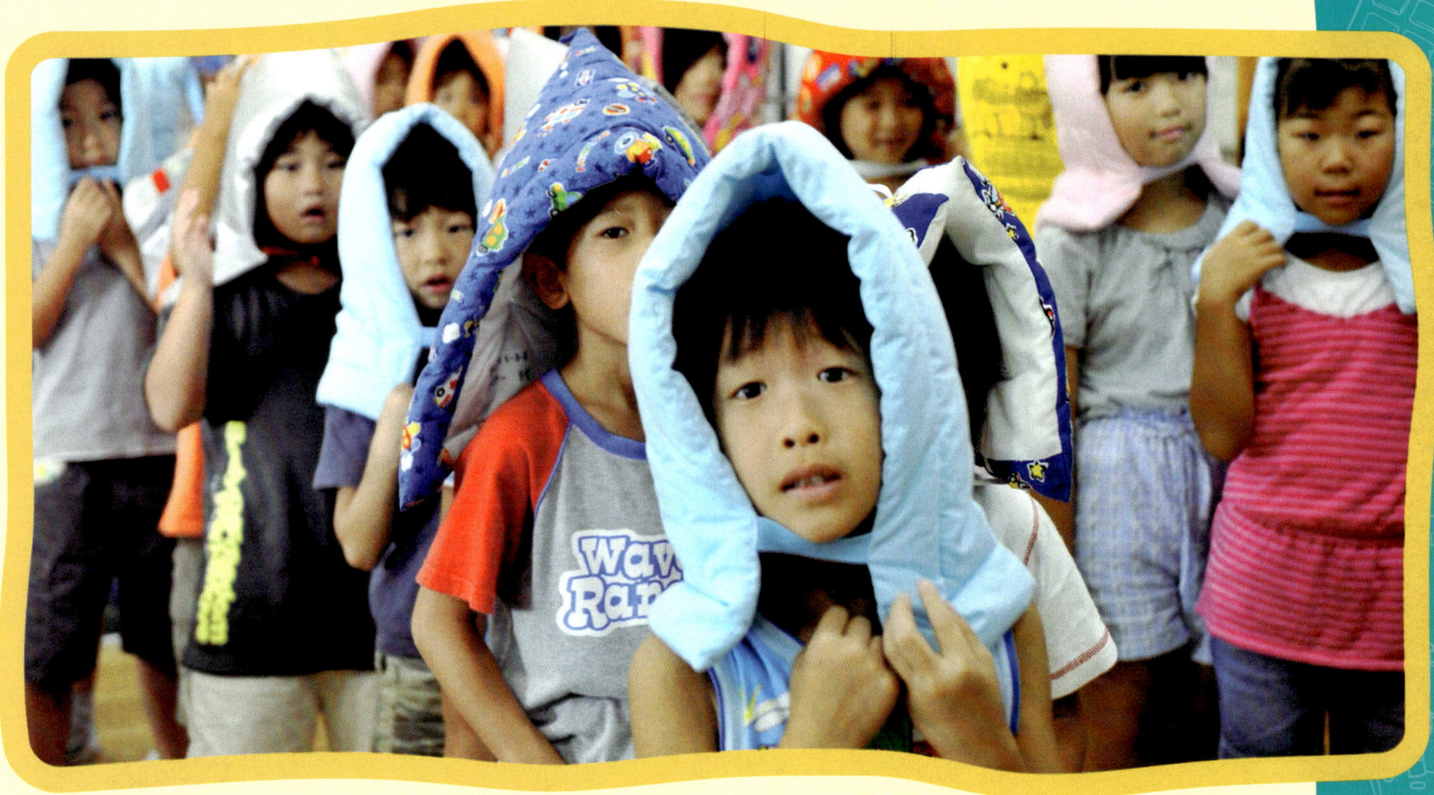

To stay safe from falling walls or ceilings, children must hide under their desks. They practice doing this during earthquake drills. They also wear padded, fireproof hoods. This teaches children what to do in case of an earthquake.

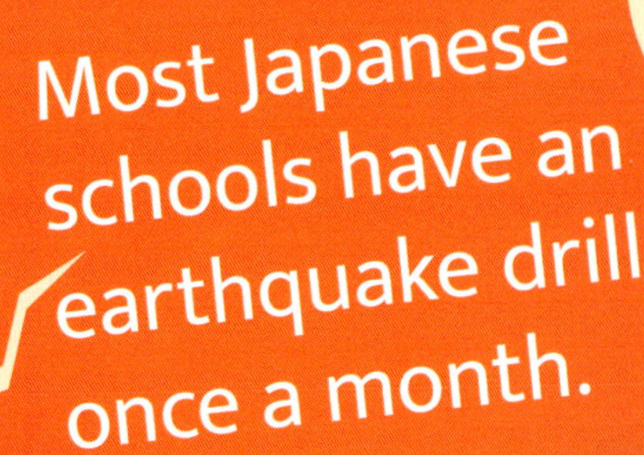

Learning on Class Trips

Lots of learning goes on outside the classroom. Children in England may go on a class trip to a farm. They learn how sheep and cattle are raised.

Schoolchildren in Kenya can visit a center for baby elephants that have lost their mothers. The babies are raised by keepers at the center. During class trips to the center, children learn about protecting elephants.

A School in a Tent

In 2011, a war began in Syria. Millions of Syrian people left their homes to escape from danger. These people became refugees.

Thousands of refugees found safety at the Al Zaatari refugee camp in Jordan.

At the camp, some children get to go to school in tent classrooms.

No Time for School

Many children cannot go to school. This is because they have to go to work every day.

Children work to earn money to help their families pay for food and medical care.

Thankfully, many people are trying to help working children.

One thing that can be changed is to make bosses pay adult workers higher wages.

If parents can earn more money, their children won't have to work.

What do these schools have in common? How are they alike?

How are these schools different? Why are they different?

KEY WORDS

Research has shown that as much as 65 percent of all written material published in English is made up of 300 words. These 300 words cannot be taught using pictures or learned by sounding them out. They must be recognized by sight. This book contains 107 common sight words to help young readers improve their reading fluency and comprehension. This book also teaches young readers several important content words, such as proper nouns. These words are paired with pictures to aid in learning and improve understanding.

Page	Sight Words First Appearance
4	all, and, are, children, don't, get, in, it's, of, off, over, same, school, the, there, they, to, up, way, world
5	a, by, day, from, on, some, states
6	down, has, made, once, our, out, study, that, their, work
7	boys, girls
8	few, four, home, is, it, just, live, one, only, so, sometimes, takes, three, very
9	at, every, for, go, old, two, years
10	do, make, read, see, we, what, write
11	others
12	book, come, them, who
13	about, animals, can, carry, far, many, move, people, place, small, with
14	an, country, this
15	also, have, most, must, or, their, under
16	farm, how, learn, may
18	began, left, these
19	found
20	be, food, help, if, more, time

Page	Content Words First Appearance
4	millions , morning
5	boat, Canada, Myanmar, students, United States, yellow buses
6	branches, classrooms, dirt floor, kids, Maasai, Tanzania, walls
7	India, math
8	Canna, coast, island, mainland, pupils, Scotland
10	art, friends, music, science, teachers
11	chalkboard, computers, schoolwork, tablets
12	Africa, camel, Kenya, library
13	camps, nomads, towns, villages
14	buildings, damage, drills, earthquake, ground, Japan
15	ceilings, desks, fireproof hoods
16	cattle, class trips, England, sheep
17	babies, elephant, keepers
18	danger, refugees, Syria, war
19	Al Zaatari refugee camp, Jordan, safety
20	bosses, medical care, money, parents, wages, workers

Published by Smartbook Media Inc.
350 5th Avenue, 59th Floor New York, NY 10118
Website: www.openlightbox.com

Printed in the United States of America in Brainerd, Minnesota
1 2 3 4 5 6 7 8 9 0 22 21 20 19 18

012018
120117

Library of Congress Cataloging in Publication Control Number:
2017959804

ISBN 978-1-5105-3544-2 (hardcover)
ISBN 978-1-5105-3545-9 (multi-user eBook)

Project Coordinator: John Willis
Art Director: Terry Paulhus

Every reasonable effort has been made to trace ownership and to obtain permission to reprint copyright material. The publisher would be pleased to have any errors or omissions brought to its attention so that they may be corrected in subsequent printings. The publisher acknowledges Getty Images, iStock, Newscom, Alamy, and the Kenya National Library Service as its primary image suppliers for this title.